The *Words*

I'LL NEVER SAY

L. Alice Bushuyev

ISBN 979-8-88616-277-6 (paperback)
ISBN 979-8-88616-278-3 (digital)

Christian Faith Publishing
832 Park Avenue
Meadville, PA 16335
www.christianfaithpublishing.com

Printed in the United States of America

Blood runs cold,
It runs red.
She feels relief
From the pain
That she hides.
That's the day
She leaves with
A real smile
On her face.
One she doesn't
Have to fake.
She found life
In a silver blade.
Painting red
She's hurt too long.
And now
She's
GONE.

Everybody falls sometimes,
Everybody hurts.
Everybody feels the pain.
You just got to love,
You just got to trust.
Let me help you up.
    I know where you've been,
I have felt your pain,
Don't you go away
I'm right there,
I'm right here.
Let me see your pain.
    There's no need to fake a smile.
Let me be the one for you
Let me be the one to show you
the truth.
I'll be here to love
I'll be here to cherish you,
Just know you are never alone.
We are a family,
Family cares, and so do we.
Just stay with me.

You say that you love me,
That I deserve better,
That I would be better off without you.
But you don't understand
That I love you
That to me,
you ARE the best
That without you, I'm dead.
The voices tell you lies.
That you don't belong,
That you're better off dead,
That you'll be doing everyone a favor by leaving.
Let me remind you,
The voices lie.
You are needed more than you think you are.
You are wanted here,
        By a lot of people
I'll end this piece by saying,

I LOVE YOU
And wish that you were here.

It shocks me that when I have my glasses on,
They don't see the pain.
They don't see how numb I am.
They don't see the emptiness I feel.
When the glasses come off
And they see the redness
And the under-eye circles
They STILL don't ask what's wrong.
Now days the question
"How are you?"
Is now just common courtesy.
No one really cares,
No one REALLY wants to know.
You just say
"I'm good"
Or
"I'm tired"
And they believe you
The smile on your face
Covers up the feelings in your heart
The voices in your head
They think you really ARE good,
You smile when you talk,
You smile through the day.
If they would look into
Your eyes when you talk or smile…
They will see the pain
You hide so well.

But they don't
And you feel
You aren't needed,
You aren't wanted
That you are   alone
So you pull the trigger,
Tie the noose,
Take the pills,
Slide the blade,
And   bleed to
death
Only THEN they notice,
And they regret,
For not paying attention...
They start regretting...
And feeling guilty...
They get depressed...
And
              join
                              you.

I need to know that you're alive
I need to tell you my "I love you"
I need to hear your voice again
I need to hear you call me "princess"
You are my prince charming
You are my king
You are the one for me
You said you'll never leave.
Why do you do what you do?
Why do you say what you say?
Why do you think the thoughts you think?
Why do you love me the way that you do?
I feel guilty for making you scared.
I feel guilty for being so calm.
I feel guilty for making you worry.
I did not leave you,
I never will leave you.
I will be there soon.
Just keep fighting, my king.
You know we can do this.

Right Where You Need Me

I see the pain that's in your eyes,
I hear that helpless cry.
I know the night
Is when you feel the worst.
But don't you worry,
Don't you fret…
Give me a call,
In the middle of the night,
In the early morn
Mid-day…
Call me up.
I don't mind.
I'll be there for ya.
If you ever need a helping hand,
A leaning wall,
A listening ear…
I'll be right here
I will find a way
To buy a ticket for a plane
And fly to you, before you leave
And make us cry.

I Wanna Be...

I wanna be the light
In your darkness.
I want to be the compass
        that guides your way,
The rightful mirror
That shows the real you
Without the judgment of society.
I will show your real you
The beauty that you are.
Will you let me show you
The way to self-acceptance?

Your eyes were made so you can see the beauty that's around
Your ears were made so you can hear
The world around praising God.
Your nose to smell the roses on your walk.
Your hair adorns your face and makes the features prominent.
Your face makes you whole.
It shows emotion,
Helps you talk and share.
Your body is perfection.
Made of different parts.
Your arms, like branches,
Move around and help you eat.
Your breasts, no matter how large or small, are perfect.
Your stomach might be sticking out or caving in…
But life it does possess.
Your butt is perfect—what girl doesn't envy her friend's rounded rump?
Your legs are perfect
Whether you have a   gap
Or not.
All in all,
You are perfect through and through.
Enjoy and take pride of what you look like,
For there is not a single person that looks just like you.

Princess Emily

She was their little princess
As princesses should be.
A little spoiled…
A little stubborn…
But she was sweet.
A bit naïve,
She fell too hard
And broke too fast.
She met a lad
Who seemed to be sweet.
When one day she took her mom and went to see the lad.
While Mother watched,
He held her close.
As soon as Mother looked away,
He hit their little girl.
The princess whimpered
from her pain with every bruise
When Mommy tried to pull her child 'way,
She hid in his room…
Where he locked her in the closet…
With no way to get to her princess
The mother calls her best friend
In hopes that she will help.

A Helping Hand

You   r   e   a   c   h   to me, but I don't
hear.
You call, but I don't listen.
I fall and break
And look around to find a helping hand.
Seeing no one is around,
I feel worthless,
Not needed,
And I repent.
I cry in anguish…
Right around my breaking point,
I look up and see a hand.
A hand that lifts me up
And pulls me close, saying,
"Child, abide my laws.
Don't walk away
Thinking you know best."
I watch and wait
To see your face again
To hear that sweet, sweet voice,
"Child, stay with me."

I'm Sorry

I'm sorry for the broken trust
I'm sorry for unspoken words.
I'm sorry
I'm sorry that I made you cry
I'm sorry that I hurt you
I'm sorry
I'm sorry I am not the best
Go pick out from the rest
I'm sorry for my mistakes
I'm sorry for the heartbreaks
I'm sorry
Never did my mind
Think of replacing you
I'm sorry for the misunderstandings
I'm sorry for the miscommunications
I'm sorry
I will tell you over and over
"I'm sorry"
I will always mean it
And always regret my mistakes
I LOVE YOU

Doll

I've become a shell of a person
Got no feeling
Got no strength
All these days, there's no energy
No motivation to do anything.
I'm a doll
You see me move
I have all body parts,
I get dressed,
Smile and wave
But inside I'm hollow
Filled with air
      f   l   o   a   t   i   n   g
I'm here just   on
a cloud
Day to day
I don't know how I feel
Can't even close my eyes
Without seeing my spinout happen.
Nights turn to day
I lie awake in bed
Just wishing things were different
That *I* was different

You say that
Life is what you make it out to be
But is it really?
Is there no God?
The supreme power that knows your life ahead of time?
Even if to others and to you
It seems like you threw a curveball
Or a plot twist…
He knew your life would happen
Like it happened
Nothing new you do
Has not been seen ahead by God
It's always Him
To Him be praise and Glory
Forever and Amen

Day of Atonement

A day of fasting
That happens once a year.
No food or water.
It's a day when some rejoice
No one forces you to eat
In fact, when they see you have WATER
Some may try to stop you.
Only sounds you hear
Are the rumbles of stomachs
A day to fill your spirit
Reading the Word of the Lord
No physical energy used all day.
The things you did,
Not knowing they were sins,
Are forgiven and forgotten.
That evening you can eat,
Just try not to overstuff yourself
To stay away from stomachaches

He was handsome and happy
Until they broke him.
They were shallow
Wanted just one thing.
He never heard from them after.
His father passed away
And this boy became sad.
He lost the spark in life.
His smile now just *a shadow*...
He met this girl
She wasn't like the rest,
She had baggage of her own
But she promised to always be there for him
And she was.
Until one day...
When he wanted to take his life
She broke her promise
And wasn't there
When he needed her the most.
She came too late
And he was gone.

Two weeks later
She heard from him,
He was in the hospital
She was so happy he was still alive!

Two months pass
And she hears
His sister is in the hospital.
She had a serious disease,
He was worried for her life.

Never leaving her side,
Just to come home and change...
The pain in his heart
Was felt by the girl.
She wishes to be there and comfort him
With the ocean separating the two
And the traveling expenses being much too high...
It's hard to do so.
But she wants him to know
"I'm here for you still"
Plenty of times
She's broken the trust that they had
But she never left.
Not even once
Did he leave her thoughts.
She wishes to at least just once
Put her arms around him
Take the pain away,
If only for a little while...
Here's to "one day"
One day, all the pain will be forgotten and gone.
The girl's goal is to
One day make him forget
The pain
And become the happy person that he was before all the
pain set in.

Who Are You?

Who are you when I'm not looking?
What do you REALLY feel
When you say that you're okay?
You hide your eyes
So I don't see the pain inside.
Don't hide your feelings,
Let me in so I can see…
Break the walls down
It's okay not to feel okay.
The tears,
They speak volumes.
Louder than your words.
What do you do when I'm not near?
Do you think of me?
Do you wish that I would stay?

Home

I wrap my arms around you
And it feels like home.
Your voice is soothing and calming
It's almost like coming home.
The way you look
So put together,
The way you smell
The way you feel,
It all just makes me feel at home
When I'm with you,
You are my home.

Home is where the heart is.

Love Letter That You'll Never See

Your smile,
Your eyes,
Your hair,
Your laugh,
Make me fall deeper and deeper in love with you.
I'm head over heels
Waiting for you to be ready
To take the step you've been fighting yourself for quite some time.
Really hope I'm not making things harder for you.
Each time I see you,
My heart beats faster.
I hope you don't see the blush on my face
And the longing in my eyes.

Bleeding Paper Heart

I am not a fragile heart of glass
That will shatter and break
My heart is paper thin
It has been ripped apart
And bandaged over and over
There's so much pain within me
The past has left my paper heart bleeding
Each drop off blood d

                    r
                    i
                    p
                    p
                    i
                    n
                    g

Resembles each mistake I've made
One day all that will be left
Will be ashes
And I will be gone.

Another Heartbreak

I don't want another heartbreak
I don't want to repeat the same mistakes
I don't need another reason to cry
So I'm turning my phone off
And deleting our messages.
I can't keep breaking my heart,
Talking to you
Change the number on my phone
To get you out my system.

Fighting My Thoughts

It's 2 o'clock and I know
I should be sleeping.
Yet here I am,
Still awake,
Trying to rid my mind of the thoughts that make me go
mad.
The thoughts that tell me
I'm *not* good enough
I'm not worth anything
I'm not loved
I'm not wanted or needed
And so much more…
Chasing those thoughts away
Exhaust me by 3 or 4
So I can finally sleep by then.
Alarm goes off at 6 or 7
Guess coffee is the way to go.

They chose murder
Over the Savior.
One who took lives
Over one who gave them life.
The blood of the Lamb
Now rests on their hands.
From generation to generation
The blame is passed.
Yet that blood
Is the blood that once saved you and I.

Wearing glasses but
Still seeing blurry
The letters are swimming
In front of my face.
Even after being asleep
For 12 hours.
My eyes involuntarily close.
Spots all around
Cover the page.
Thinking, "How am I alive?"
Sermon of fearing God
Realizing where I started going wrong.
Once you start thinking
What others think of you,
You start trying to please them more than God.
You lose yourself.
FEAR GOD AND LET MEN LAUGH.

The crisp air outside
Makes me think of renewal
Just like the world goes through
The cold, hard winter
Freezing and dying
Becoming fragile and breaking
So do we.
We go from strong to weak
From recovery to relapse
All of that is just part of a roller coaster called life
There are ups and downs in life.
We just need to KEEP fighting and get back up when you fall.

Running

Running from the good
But running to the bad.
Instead of helping ourselves
We surround ourselves
With those who kill us inside.
You know the "bad for you" kind of people
That you,
Delusionally,
Think will turn good for you.
They won't change.
The only one they CAN change
Is YOU.
You will lose yourself in their bad ways.

It's been a while since we've been together,
But it's nice to know that we're still close.
We can talk about the most random things
Yet have a serious conversation within a minute.
Close heart-to-heart talks
Bring us close.
The fun little moments
Remind that we're still kids.
It's so easy to tell you
All that I do…
I'm shocked that knowing all you know,
You still are here.
Most people don't know even 5% of what you know
And leave
Glad to know you have my back
As much as I have yours.

Best Friend

A best friend is a treasure
One that's truly happy,
One who knows
All your thoughts and secrets
Yet stays with you until the end.
You don't need to believe in soul mates
Just know the one you're meant to have
Will be yours until the end of time.
You don't need a relationship
Just keep them close
You won't regret having them in your life
And love them unconditionally.

Prayer

Hear my plea, Lord.
Hear my cry.
Don't let me slip.
Don't let me fall.
My head hurts from all the tension,
My eyes—bloodshot from the tears threatening to spill
My heart's in shreds
My smile's fake
I'm falling back to where I was.
My old habits—sneaking into my thoughts
Telling me all will disappear.
I don't want to believe
That the pain is all I'll ever have.
Bring me back to life.
Let me see the sun shine again.
Lord, let me feel Your love
And Your power once again.
I need You now.
Please save me.

First Three Members

The first three members of the church
Were of very sinful nature:
A terrorist
A wizard
And a eunuch
All found love in the one who saved them.
These days, we all are plastic with painted-on smiles,
Acting as if we never fell,
Never hurt,
Never do wrong.
Yet we ALL fall
We all are fake
We all join forces to teach the truth of God
Without knowing, living, breathing Him.

Feel

All I want
Is to feel
Love and affection.
I'd give anything and everything
To feel any emotion
Other than numb and lonely.
I may always be surrounded
By friends and family,
And yet
I always feel alone.
My heart is pounding
Eyes are shutting.
I'm wishing for at least 12 hours of sleep for 2-3 days.
I'm tired.
Tired physically and emotionally.
I'm dreaming of one day
Waking up after a good night's sleep.
Roll over and see
The love of my life
Smiling at me.
That will be the day I say,
"I made it."

People see you as a jerk
I see you as a straight-up kind of guy
You say it like it is
No sugarcoating lies.
Straight up truth is the way you roll
And I admire you for that.
The sarcasm covers you up,
But inside
Is a sweet guy
Who knows his worth
And won't ever settle for less.
I now know why you said
That I've never been on the receiving end of your glare.
You always look away when you are mad
And never look at me unless to smile.
Thank you for all of that and more.

Silent tears
Fall as I remember my past
Thinking back
I wonder why and how I went wrong.
Where did I fall?
I used to pride myself
On being a "good churchgoing girl"
Then came the time
When I just came to church and cried.
Now I'm at church
But my mind is filled to the brim of reminders of my past

I miss our talks,
The way they lasted all night.
I miss the teasing,
The way you'd make fun of me for all the silly things.
I miss your hugs,
The simplicity of our life.
It hurts to know,
Now you are with her.
The one I spilled my heart out,
Is with the one that kills me with her eyes.
I'm happy that you found she makes you happy
I pray her heart doesn't break.
If that does happen,
Let me know…
Or don't.
Knowing them,
They'll blame it all on me.
I'll be your sideline girl.
The one who sticks around forever.
May God forever keep your heart happy.

When everything falls apart
I fall back to You.
You know my past, present, and future.
You know where I've been…
You know what I've done,
And yet
You love me just the same.
Your love
Is unconditional.
It never fails,
Never leaves.
I know You still are by my side.
You're coming near to hold me.
Through my pain,
I feel Your love surround me.
I thank You, Lord,
For being here with me,
For loving me,
And keeping me alive.

02/25/2016

When you think your life is going good,
Don't forget about a greater thing.
The thing called gravity,
Everything that's up
Must come down.
Going up and feel great,
But life slaps you to reality
And brings you back down.
Don't forget to check the ground
When you're on high
To make sure you'll have a soft landing
And when you fall,
Won't break a bone.

When you try to psych me out
And try to get in my head...
You will get lost in the turmoil
You might understand
Why I am the way I am
Or
You just might try to judge me
Because you "had it worse"
Give me a break and shut your mouth.
Until you walk a mile in my shoes
You have no right
To tell me what or how to do.

Isaiah 21:11–12

Watchman, what is left of the night?
The watchman replies, "Morning is
coming, but also the night..."

Wish we could turn back time
To the good old days
When our momma sang us to sleep
But now we're stressed out.

I remember being careless, free, and wild.
When we ran around smiling, laughing
When the tears only came out
Because we fell and someone laughed.
Our biggest worry was
Our crush finding out that we liked them.
Can we go back to that time
So we don't have to feel the pain
That our thoughts bring us?
The subconscious pain sinks us down into darkness of depression.
I want to be able to laugh and smile.
I want to feel the rush of the wind
Making me feel careless, wild, and free.

Days are long
Nights grow short and cold
Without you there to share them with.

I miss hearing your voice
I miss seeing your face
I'm sorry for the mess I made

I didn't think it'd snowball this far
I didn't want you to leave the house.
Can you forgive me for these two months of torture in
your life?

I hate this entry. It sucks. BLAH.

We gotta live like we are dying tomorrow
Do the things
That, looking back,
We won't regret.
Be a kid at heart,
Ignore what people think
Just be you.
Stay true to you.
Screw society.
You'll never make you happy
If you try to make society happy.
It's controversial within itself.
So just be YOU.
You're the best YOU
You can ever be.

Forgiveness

It's so easy to talk about forgiving and forgetting.
But to actually practice the act…
Forgiving ourselves and forgetting our mistakes
Is the hardest thing to do.
How do you forgive,
Let alone FORGET, your own mistakes?
There's so much I wish I didn't do.
Unfortunately,
You can't undo life
And the choices that have lifelong consequences.
It's how we learn
And live after we mess up.

There's a war raging inside of me
The demons
Cast away…
Trying to break my door of confidence
Sending thoughts of doubt.
Telling me they never left
That I'm just blocking them out.
I almost fell back
Into the same patterns several days ago.
Standing straight,
Upright,
Standing strong
Is harder after faking it for so long.
My breathing is becoming labored
Though my heart feels fear,
My thoughts are going haywire,
Hoping they straighten out.

Filling up this book,
Filling it up page by page…
Trying to get all my mess out on these pages.
Wanting to start a new book
A new life.
Tell me why my legs are spasming
Why my arms feel as if someone is dragging blades across them.
I'm half-expecting to see my sleeves soaked with blood.
Part of me
Hopes that this pain will subside.
Page by page,
Filling this book with pain
Filling it with hurtful words.
Years from now,
Wanting to look back to see how far I got.
Hoping all this pain will stay in the past and not follow me into the future.

Mercy

I feel your mercy, O God.
I don't deserve
The mercy You pour out.
Each day I wake up
And am amazed.
Amazed that You still love me.
ME—the one that put up a front.
ME—the one who faked her way.
But You… You alone are just.
You know my path,
You know my pain,
You were there next to me.
Saw my sins…
Yet…
Died for me
To save me.
Save me from myself.
Your mercy—the only thing that keeps me living.

Hypocrisy

We look so nice,
Dressed up and fancy.
We sit straight,
Make it seem like we are listening,
Yet most of the time
We sit and judge the ones around us.
From what they wear,
To how you talk in church.
From how you walk,
To what you do when you are out.
They think of your past,
The mistakes that you've made.
We say the "right" things
Act the "right" way
But try and spot us any other day.
You'll never know who we are.
For once out of the church
We melt, mold into different people
Those who look just like you.

Yesterday

Yesterday brought back feelings
Feelings that have been gone.
Seeing my shirt
Tossed behind the toilet—
Used for other things it's not intended for.
Got me feeling disgusted more than when I was in his shoes.
Breaks my heart
That even after I've been redeemed,
The disgust still shadows over me.
I can't even look at him straight
Without thinking what he does behind our backs.
Why is it the people who are supposed to make you feel safe
Are the ones who violate you the most?
I don't understand at all.

Finally, brothers, whatever is true, whatever is noble, whatever is right, whatever is pure, whatever is lovely, whatever is admirable—if anything is excellent or praiseworthy—think about such things. Whatever you have learned from me—put it in practice. And the God of peace will be with you.

—Philippians 4:8–9

06/25/2016

How wonderful, merciful, perfect, and amazing
Is God's power.
His love endures forever.
He sees us at our worst,
And yet He loves us,
Tries to make us see the right path.
He wants us to learn our lesson.
He might even make it seem
Like He's forgotten us…
Just to get us back into His arms.
Arms full of love and safety.

Metaphor

Walking today
I saw a metaphor
happen in front of my eyes.
I always,
When I leave the house,
Spritz a light, sweet fragrance.
I did that today out of habit,
But there were diesels
Passing by.
By the time
I reached my destination,
I smelled more of diesel
Than of fruits.
I found that
When we surround
Ourselves with God,
We smell sweet.
But as we pass by
Everyday life
And dip into the toxicity of sin,
We lose the sweetness of His love.
In your everyday life
Stay strong.
Lean on Him.
He'll get you through it.

I feel the pain returning
It's like an overwhelming flood.
Rushing, rushing
As if it thinks I can handle it.
I refuse to fall back on that path.
I will NOT fall,
For You are here with me.
I want to feel joy, love, laughter.
I feel the pain returning,
It's seeping through my bones.
God, why is this happening to me?
Let me feel You near
So I know You won't let me go.
The pain is unbearable.
You see it in my eyes
When tears come down.
You walk away,
Leaving me here to be alone.

The voices
The faces
They're all coming back
I bring my walls up
To keep them out
But there's cracks in my wall
From previous years
They sneak in through my walls
And right into my head.
I need Your protection, Lord
Let me stay safe
And not fall into the same patterns at 19
As I was at 16–18
I don't want to be that girl
That breaks,
Fakes, and takes
Everything to heart.
I want,
I need Genuine.

Red Flags

I've been warned
To stay away
For my safety
I thought you were different
I thought you'd never lay a hand,
Leave a bruise,
And have no regrets about it.
I learned to feel safe.
Safe with you…
I heard the warning threats
Never thinking you would follow through.
You got me sticking up for you
Covering for you
To keep me clean.
They tell me to forget you,
They say, "Just walk away."
But I am here…
I can't walk away
I've been warned.
But now I'm burned.

my eyes are guarded
they lost their sparkle
i'M NO LONGER CAREFREE
i GET UPSET AT THE SIMPLE THINGS
a WORD CAN SEND ME INTO OVERDRIVE
i'M FEELING WEAK
i'M ALWAYS TIRED
i CAN'T STAY AWAKE
mY EYES ARE SHUTTING
SO GUARDED
SO HEAVY
i'M GOING TO SLEEP
gOOD NIGHT

Take Me Back

Take me back to when
We were kids
Our whole life ahead
And so innocent.
We didn't know
The odds were against us
Thought the world was on our side.
Thinking highly of people
Not knowing what intentions are
Growing up, we see not all things are peachy.
Outside,
People are dying and crying
Families are breaking apart
So much pain and agony
Take me back to the innocent days
When we had love for the world
When we cared about others.
Being honest
Instead of saying the right things at the right time,
Just nodding.
Gotta be honest,
Being a child was better.

Am I being stupid?
Coming back to you
Ignoring all the pain.
Just because I see
What others can't
I know that
It's a front you put up
And not your real self.
The real you is
A momma's boy
A sweet and kind
Heart and soul
That's been hurt and used
Before—
Putting up a front
Like you don't care.
Like there is no one
Who can break down your wall.
Guess what, though?
I only annoy you
Because you know
I have the key
To break those walls.

I've been there.
I had those walls.
And I know,
Heart on my sleeve
Won't keep me safe
But it gets others
To trust me.
So...
Good luck trying
To get rid of me.
Even when I walk away,
I'm still on your mind.
Using my body not my intent
But if my body had a say,
I wouldn't turn away.

You say you want me to be happy
But the problem is
I'm scared of being happy
'Cause every time
There's a cause for happiness
Something always comes along
And ruins it for me.
To be happy in life is a dream
But I sabotage myself every time
You made me happy.
And still to this day
Are you sure you are willing to
Deal with me for much longer?
If you are really wanting to be in it for life
I am most definitely NOT against it.

With only ten pages left
I continue filling up
This book with my thoughts
And my words
Writing, writing, constantly
Writing—constantly thinking
Through the highs and the lows
I keep writing
Never stopping,
Never quitting,
Just writing
Through the cold and the heat
My thoughts keep running
I keep writing
All my thoughts
All my conflicts
All my feelings
Always writing
Filling pages one by one
Never thinking that I could
Finish this book,
One day,
So soon,
In just a year
I've filled up this book.

Pages left keep lessening
My heart is
Pounding,
Breaking, speeding up,
Not wanting to be done
My thoughts going crazy
How I've changed
Within this year is insane
Making my head hurt
From all the thoughts
And words rushing through
And being written here.

I should have known
My life was way too calm
Way too quiet
How could I forget
What happened all those days ago?
And now
He's back
I see him two rows behind me
Why am I so tense?
So scared
I almost forgot that night
Him being here
Reminded me all that
I can't go through the day
Knowing he is near
I swore to never fall
But this don't feel like falling
Gravity can't even help
The ground beneath me is gone
Now I can't breathe
I've got to go

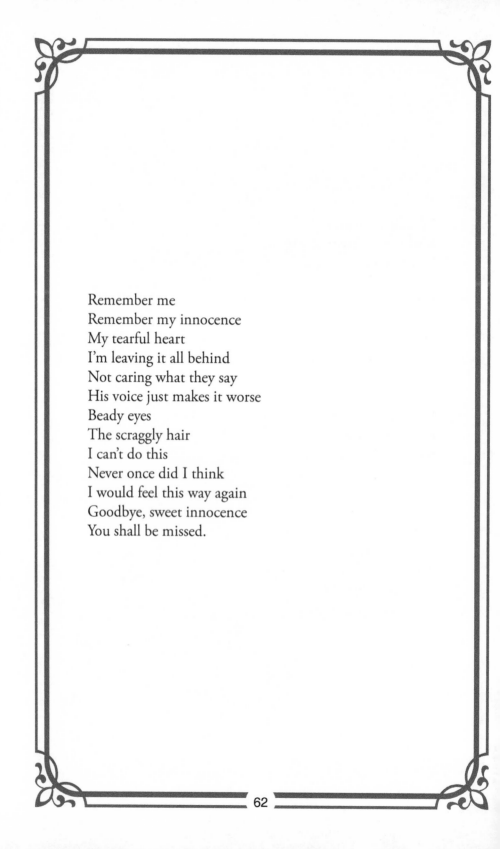

Remember me
Remember my innocence
My tearful heart
I'm leaving it all behind
Not caring what they say
His voice just makes it worse
Beady eyes
The scraggly hair
I can't do this
Never once did I think
I would feel this way again
Goodbye, sweet innocence
You shall be missed.

There's no calming me down
I'm shaking
It's hard to breathe
I feel my heart breaking
So tense
Keeping tears at bay
Is getting harder
My feet are numb now
Wish I could numb my heart now too
Would help me feel not feel this pain
How could he?!
Why would he?!
Argh!
And here comes the gut-wrenching cry
The shaky hands
I have officially given up.

With a family as broken as mine…
You expect me to do good?
No, it's not broken in the sense
That many marriages are ending in divorce—
That, honestly, would be better sometimes
But we are broken in the sense that
Our families are falling apart
But instead of divorce
They hurt each other with words
20+ years of emotional breakdowns
And you tell me to be happy?
Keep laughing?
Stay strong? How?
Where would I get such examples when all around
Are sarcasm and argument?

What Is Love?

Love is patient, love is kind. It does not envy, it does not boast, it is not proud. It is not rude, it is not self-seeking, it is not easily angered, it keeps no record of wrongs. Love does not delight in evil but rejoices with the truth. It always protects, always trusts, always hopes, always preserves. Love never fails.

—1 Corinthians 13:4–8

That is love.
Have you had it?
Have you seen it?
Is love even possible?
Why do we always talk of love
But never feel it?
Never show it?
We only know lust
And how to please ourselves.
The right here, right now is our focus.
We don't care about the future
How others feel.
We are self-centered,
Selfish, egoistical,
Sensitive people.
We get upset and offended
By the most simple things.
If a single word can offend you,
I'm sorry, your life
Will be a disappointment to you.

I am so tired of being strong
Tired of being the "good" kid
When everyone around me is
Screaming, crying, yelling...
Why do I have to be
Calm, quiet, strong, and loyal?
I'm tired of living a lie
When do I get to be me?
Live my life?
I've been living a life
That others planned for me.
Why must I follow the path
They chose for me?
I want to be me.
Yes, I'll make mistakes,
But who doesn't?
I want to break down
I want to cry
I want to feel loved
When will I get that?
Or will all my wants
Just be dreams?

I want to live a life
Where, in the end,
I can say,
"I'M DONE."
I want to travel,
Meet new people,
See the amazing sights
This planet has to offer.
I want to be able
To breathe the fresh air
That is in the open fields of the countryside,
Then come back
To see the familiar faces,
Feel the familiar hugs.
That is when I'll be able to fully and completely say,
"I LIVED."
I lived, not just survived.
Survival won't fill you.
You are just breathing because you have to.

My brother has a problem.
His problem's very clear.
My brother has a problem.
He has the need to be near.
My brother has a problem.
He needs to understand.
My brother has a problem—
That needs to hear the

        Answer NO.

The last two pages have been filled on September 3, 2016, at 7:15 p.m.

It's been an adventure, but it is time to close this book and start another.

I've had ups and downs with this book.

I'm excited to start the new one.

Thank you for keeping my memories.

I will remember you while making new ones.

With love,
Me

About the Author

As a teen who has been taught the glory of God but is still going through that teen angst, Alice set out to write her thoughts down. The words written in this book are words she thought she'd never say out loud.

Here you will find what went on in her head during the low days and the high days. She has also included some stories about her friends and people she met along the way. No names have been included to keep their identities safe, but if you've met people like the ones in here, the author suggests you read this as a warning tale of what could happen if people stray from the way of the Lord.